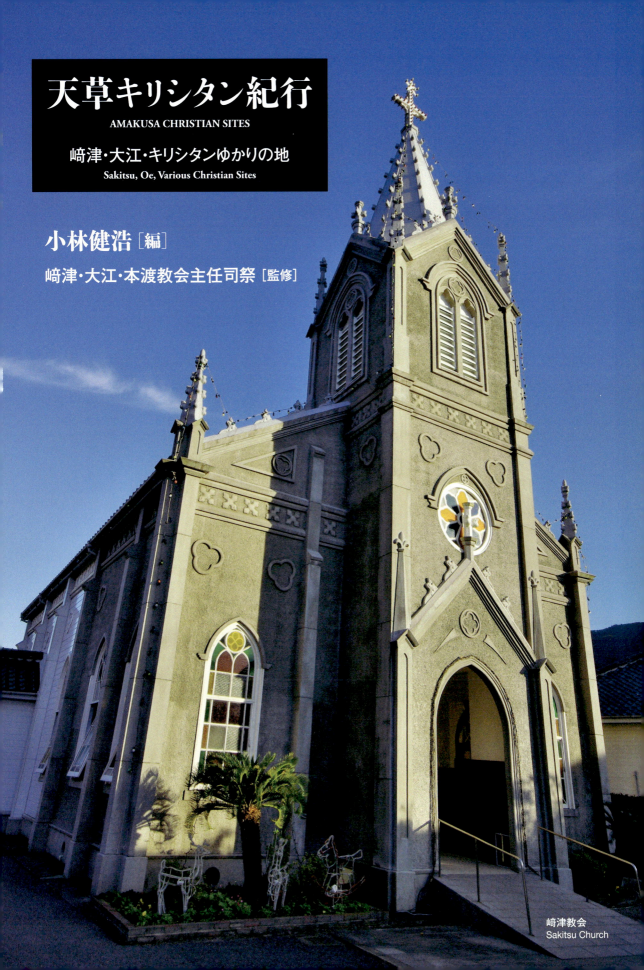

天草キリシタン紀行
AMAKUSA CHRISTIAN SITES

﨑津・大江・キリシタンゆかりの地
Sakitsu, Oe, Various Christian Sites

小林健浩［編］
﨑津・大江・本渡教会主任司祭［監修］

﨑津教会
Sakitsu Church

夜明けの﨑津　Sakitsu in the Morning

宗教法人カトリック福岡司教区
司教　宮原良治
Catholic Diocese of Fukuoka
Bishop Ryoji Miyahara

発刊によせて

　コバルトブルーの海、広葉樹におおわれた島々の緑、紺碧の空など、自然が豊かで風光明媚な天草は宝の島と呼ばれています。それは、山海の幸や自然の恵みだけでなく、歴史や文化などの精神的な遺産や宝物にも恵まれているからです。

　この度の写真集はたくさんの天草の宝物を紹介してありますが、その中でも特に、可視的で具体的な姿や形の背景にある見えない世界の富を提示して下さっています。それが、まさに数百年の歴史によって育まれた天草最大の宝物の一つである「信仰の遺産」です。私たちは、激動する社会の中で、生活の豊かさを一途に追求するあまり、便利さや快適さという目先のことに追い回され、ややもすれば本当に大事なものをどこかに置き忘れているかもしれません。

　本書は、私たちが日常の営みで置き去りにしているもの、つまり、人智を超えた方への「畏敬の念」という尊い宝物を再認識させ、本物の豊かさや真に価値ある超越的な世界に招いて下さいます。その意味で、この写真集は、より崇高で、よりけだかく、より聖なるものへの歩みをもう一度新たにさせ、「人生をかけて全うしなければならない人の道とは何か」、「不動の価値ある真理とは何か」、「いのちの本当の豊かさとは何か」という問い掛けに対する思いを再認識させて下さる素晴らしい企画だと思います。

Forward

With its cobalt blue sea, azure sky, and broad leafed trees coloring the islands green, Amakusa is called Treasure Island. We are blessed not only with its abundant scenery of mountains and seascapes, but are also blessed with the spiritual treasures of its history and culture.

Many of Amakusa's treasures are introduced in this collection of photographs. The greatest of these treasures is the "legacy of faith" that has been nurtured through a history of several hundred years. In particular, these pages provide insights into a world of unseen treasures that lie beneath the surface of what is tangible. We live in a tumultuous world in which our single focus is on acquiring wealth. We are preoccupied with the pursuit of what is pleasurable and convenient. It seems to be our nature to lose sight of what is truly important.

This book helps us to take a fresh look at true wealth and real treasures that get left behind in everyday life, and invites us to ponder with a sense of awe the person who transcends human understanding. In this sense, "Amakusa Christian Sites" is a splendid work that calls us to more noble, more lofty, and more saintly ways to reexamine the questions of: What should we accomplish in our life? What is immutable truth? and What is true wealth in life?

「島の祈り」

天草こころの旅

秘めた祈り
感謝の祈り
少しばかりの懺悔(ざんげ)の祈り
そして明日への祈り

静かにこころを開く
天草こころの旅

Pilgrimage in Amakusa

  We pray in silence
  We pray in thanks
  We pray for forgiveness
  We pray for tomorrow

 In the silence we open our hearts and minds
 Pilgrimage in Amakusa

目次 / TABLE OF CONTENTS

04	序文	Forward

写真編 / PHOTOGRAPHS

- 07 﨑津教会とその周辺 — Sakitsu Church and Nearby
- 27 大江教会とその周辺 — Oe Church and Nearby
- 37 キリシタンゆかりの地 — Other Christian Sites
  - ●根引の子部屋 ●富岡城趾とアダム荒川殉教地 ●鬼の城キリシタン墓碑公園 ●ペーが墓 ●殉教公園 ●祇園橋 ●本渡教会 ●コレジヨ公園 ●正覚寺（南蛮寺跡） ●湯島
  - ● Nebiki Site ● Tomioka Castle and Adam-Arakawa's Martyrdom ● Onnojo Christian Grave Yard ● Pe's Grave ● Martyrdom Park ● Gionbashi Bridge ● Hondo Church ● Colegio Park ● Shokakuji Temple ● Yushima Island
- 51 ミサ — Mass
- 59 シスター — Sisters
- 61 祭礼 — Festivals
- 65 キリスト教天草伝来450年祭 — 450th Anniversary Ceremony
- 68 偉人たちの肖像 — Historical Figures
  - ●ハルブ神父 ●ガルニエ神父 ●フェリエ神父 ●アダム荒川 ●アルメイダ ●天草四郎
  - ● Father Halbout ● Father Garnier ● Father Ferrier ● Adam Arakawa ● Luis de Almeida ● Shiro Amakusa
- 70 弾圧と潜伏の時代 — The Time of Persecution and Hiding

資料編 / APPENDICES

- 73 天草の思いを世界へ — From Amakusa to the World
- 76 天草のキリスト教史 — Amakusa's Christian History
- 80 世界遺産の﨑津集落 — World Heritage Status of Sakitsu Village
- 85 天草のキリスト教年表 — Chronology of Amakusa's Christianity History
- 87 資料館の案内 — Guide of Museums
  - ●天草キリシタン館 ●天草コレジヨ館 ●天草ロザリオ館 ●﨑津資料館みなと屋 ●サンタマリア館 ●苓北町歴史資料館 ●天草四郎メモリアルホール
  - ● Amakusa Christian Museum ● Amakusa Colegio Museum ● Amakusa Rosary Museum ● Sakitsu Museum Minatoya ● Amakusa Chrisao Museum ● Reihoku Historical Museum ● Amakusa Shiro Memorial Hall

その他 / OTHER

- 94 案内地図 — Guide Maps
- 97 協力者一覧とあとがき — Epiloque

・保有者の記載のない写真は小林健浩の撮影
・資料編の画像は主に天草市や各資料館の提供
・表紙カバーの写真は﨑津
・裏表紙カバーの写真は大江教会

・Photos without name are taken by Takehiro Kobayashi
・Pictorial images in APPENDICES are mainly provided by Amakusa city and each Museum
・Photo on front cover sheet is Sakitsu
・Photo on rear cover sheet is Oe Church

﨑津教会とその周辺
Sakitsu Church and Nearby

© Carl Jenson

﨑津鳥瞰① Aerial View ①

© Carl Jenson

﨑津鳥瞰② Aerial View ②

﨑津集落　Sakitsu Village

Ⓒ（一社）天草宝島観光協会　　　﨑津鳥瞰③　Aerial View ③

Ⓒ Carl Jenson　　　﨑津鳥瞰④　Aerial View ④

旧祭壇　Old Altar

夜の彩り　Illuminated Stained Glass

祭壇は弾圧期に絵踏みが行われた場所に建てられている
The altar is located on the place where *Efumi* was carried out during the years of persecution.

クリスマス イヴ　Christmas Eve

春の﨑津
Sakitsu in Spring

冬の﨑津
Sakitsu in Winter

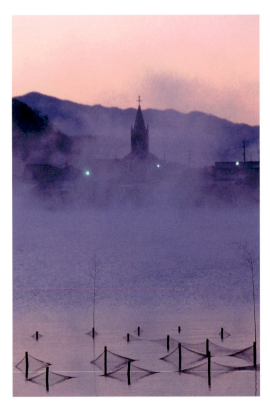

海のマリア像
Bayside Statue of Mary

港の出口に立つマリア像は航海の安全を祈っている
Mary watches over ships going out to sea.

夕暮れ①　Sunset ①

ご安全に　Praying for Safe Fishing

ⓒ 永田隆一

夕暮れ②　Sunset ②

キリシタン墓地
Christian Graves

静かに眠る   Rest in Peace

海を見下ろす   Overlooking the Sea

累代の墓   Graveyard

カケの光景 / View of Kake

カケとは﨑津独特の造りで、いわば海からの玄関口であり、物干しや網の繕いなどの生活の場になっている
Kake is a kind of seafront porch used for tasks such as drying fish or mending nets.

チャペルの丘 / Chapel Hill

チャペルの丘からは眺望が良い
We can see a nice view from here.

﨑津諏訪神社
Sakitsu Suwa Shrine

教会のすぐ近くに神社がある。弾圧の時代、信者はここで祈らされた
Hidden Christians prayed here in secret. They prayed in public with others but prayed to "God" in their hearts.

﨑津諏訪神社から　From Sakitsu Suwa Shrine

﨑津諏訪神社　Sakitsu Suwa Shrine

今富集落 Imatomi Village

今富集落は隠れキリシタンの里として知られる
Imatomi Village is known as a place where Hidden Christians lived and have kept their faith to this day.

古い教会跡　Site of Church Ruins

ⓒ 熊本日日新聞社

臼飾り　今富地区に伝わるキリシタンの新年を迎える風習
Usukazari　This custom from Hidden Christians is still practiced for greeting the new year.

大山大神宮（十五社宮）のマリア風石像
Stone Mary-like Statue in Shrine

暮らし
Daily Life

家庭祭壇　Home Altar

夕べの祈り　Evening Prayer

手入れ　Repairing Nets

漁船の中の祭壇
Altar in a Fishing Boat

帰港　Returning to Port

干物づくり　Making Dried Fish

貝掘り　Digging for Clams

「トウヤ」と呼ばれる路地　Alley Called *Toya*

干物づくり Making Dried Fish

登校 Going to School

大江教会とその周辺
Oe Church and Nearby

薄暮の大江教会　Oe Church at Dusk

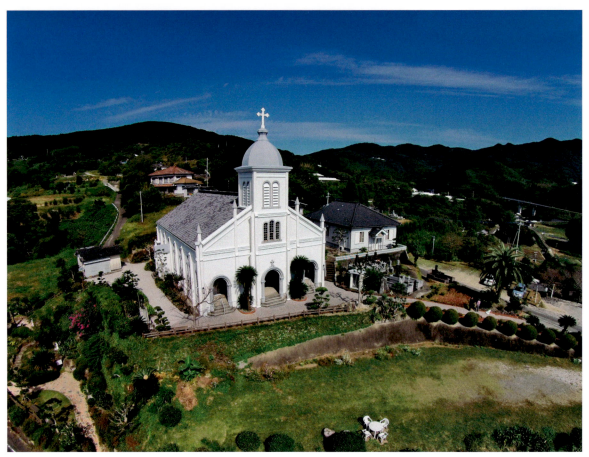

© Carl Jenson   大江鳥瞰① Aerial View ①

© Carl Jenson   大江鳥瞰② Aerial View ②

大江教会正面　Front of the Oe Church

大江教会裏面　Back of the Oe Church

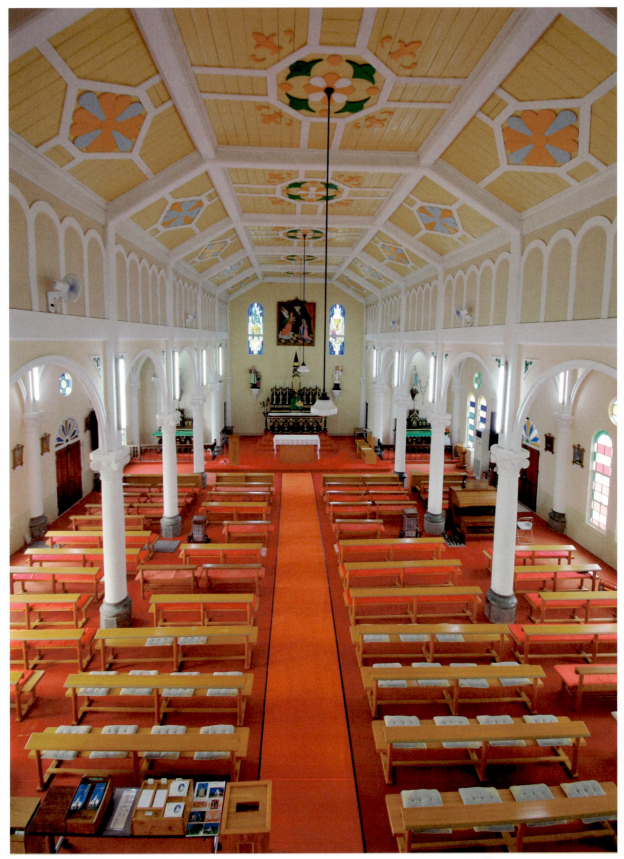

礼拝堂　Inside of the Oe Church

夜の彩り　Illuminated Stained Glass

ⓒ 永田隆一　　　　　　　　　　　　　　　　　　　夜の大江教会　Oe Church at Night

ガルニエ神父像　Father Garnier

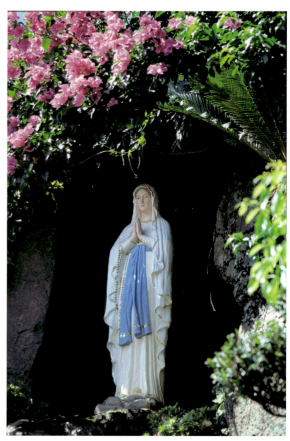
マリア像①　Statue of Mary ①

マリア像②　Statue of Mary ②

雨の墓地　Grave on a Rainy Day

西平キリシタン墓地
Grave in Nishibira

カノコユリ咲く　Lilies in Bloom

夕暮れ　Sunset

暮らし
Daily Life

家庭祭壇　Home Altar

祈り　Offering Prayers

家庭祭壇　Home Altar

歴史を語る祭壇　Altar Showing Faith History

農作業① Farming ①

農作業② Farming ②

根引の子部屋 / Nebiki Site

フェリエ神父が開設した孤児院等の施設で根引の深い山中にあった。
春には「十字架の道行」が行われる

There was formerly an orphanage in Nebiki established by Father Ferrier. "Stations of the Cross" are held on Good Friday.

十字架の道行き① Stations of the Cross ①

十字架の道行き② Stations of the Cross ②

崇敬 Veneration of the Cross

悲しみのマリア　Sorrowful Mary

標石　One of the 14 Stations

﨑津教会遠望　View to Sakitsu Church

富岡城趾とアダム荒川殉教地
Tomioka Castle and Site of Adam Arakawa's Martyrdom

富岡城は天草四郎の率いる一揆軍が落とせなかった強固な城。
アダム荒川は拷問を受けこの一角で殉教した
Shiro Amakusa attacked this castle, but was unsuccessful.
Adam Arakawa was martyred here.

© Carl Jenson　富岡城趾鳥瞰　Aerial View

富岡城趾遠望　Looking Toward Tomioka Castle

アダム荒川殉教地　Site of Adam Arakawa's Martyrdom

鬼の城キリシタン墓碑公園
Onnojo Christian Grave Park
散在するキリシタン墓石を集め公園化されている
Many Christian graves were moved to this park.

春　Spring

夏　Summer

秋　Fall

冬　Winter

夜の公園　Graveyard at Night

ぺーが墓
Pe's Grave

ここは数少ない現存するキリシタン墓地。「ぺー」とは神父を意味するものと推察されている
These are authentic graves. "Pe" is a name attributed to a priest.

| 殉教公園 Martyrdom Park | ここにはキリシタン館や千人塚など様々な施設がある
At this place are the Christian Museum, *Senninzuka* (memorial mound of many people,) and other Christian sites. |

Ⓒ 天草市 キリシタン館鳥瞰 Aerial View of the Christian Museum

雪の千人塚 *Senninzuka* in Snow

キリスト像　Statue of Jesus

天草四郎像　Statue of Shiro Amakusa

Ⓒ 天草キリシタン館　陣中旗　War Banner of Shiro Amakusa

アルメイダ（レリーフ）　Luis de Almeida（Relief）

キリシタン墓碑　Christian Graveyard

祈りの人（灯籠）　Praying Figure (Engraved on Stone Lantern)

祇園橋 Gionbashi Bridge

祇園橋付近は天草四郎軍と富岡番代軍の激戦地になった
Amakusa Shiro's army fought near this bridge.

祇園橋① Gionbashi Bridge ①

祇園橋② Gionbashi Bridge ②

本渡教会 Hondo Church

昭和26年聖コロンバン会によって建立された。日曜日のミサでは大勢の信者が祈る
This church was established by the Society of St. Columban in 1951. Many Christians attend Mass here every Sunday.

外観　Front of the Hondo Church

四旬節の十字架　Lenten Crosses

コレジヨ公園 / Colegio Park

天草にコレジヨ（神父を育てる大神学校）があったが、この地とも推定されている
This place is regarded as the site of the Amakusa Christian Colegio.

春　In Spring

ライトアップ　Light Up

正覚寺（南蛮寺跡） Shokakuji Temple

かつては教会（南蛮寺）だった
There was formerly a church here.

山門　Gate

キリシタン墓石　Christian Grave Stones

湯島　Yushima Island　天草四郎ら一揆軍が作戦会議を行った島。別名談合島
Amakusa Shiro's army made battle plans on this island.

虹立つ島　Rainbow over Yushima Island

© Carl Jenson

湯島鳥瞰　Aerial View

談合碑　Monument of Battle Meeting

ミサ（クリスマス イヴ ＆ クリスマス）
Christmas Eve Mass & Christmas Mass

聖体拝領（﨑津教会）　Holy Communion（Sakitsu Church）

ⓒ Carl Jenson　　　　　　　　入祭（大江教会）　Making the Entrance（Oe Church）

栄光の賛歌①（大江教会）　Hymns of Glory ①（Oe Church）

栄光の賛歌②　Hymns of Glory ②

栄光の賛歌③　Hymns of Glory ③

説教（﨑津教会）
Homily (Sakitsu Church)

祈り　Offering Prayers

畳での祈り　Praying on *Tatami* Floor

聖体拝領（﨑津教会） Receiving Communion（Sakitsu Church）

聖歌合唱（大江教会） Singing Hymns（Oe Church）

献金（﨑津教会） Offertory（Sakitsu Church）

ミサ
Mass

祈り　Offering Prayers

ミサ① Mass ①

ミサ② Mass ②

ミサ③ Mass ③

ミサ④ Mass ④

本渡教会　Hondo Church

ⓒ Carl Jenson　　　説教（川上神父）　Homily（Father Kawaue）

ⓒ Carl Jenson　　　洗礼式　Baptism

堅信式　Confirmation
堅信式では洗礼を受けた信者が聖霊の刻印を受ける
At Confirmation Catholics are sealed with the Holy Spirit.

ⓒ 大江教会　　　宮原司教による堅信式（大江教会）
Confirmation by Bishop Miyahara（Oe Church）

四旬節黙想会
Lenten Retreat

本渡教会　Hondo Church

説教（山頭神父）　Homily（Father Yamagashira）

本渡教会で　At the Hondo Church

﨑津教会で　At the Sakitsu Church

シスター	3名のシスターが大江教会と﨑津教会で奉仕している
Sisters	Three sisters are serving in Oe and Sakitsu Church.

渡辺神父と（大江教会）　With Father Watanabe（Oe Church）

裏庭にて（大江教会）　At the Back of the Oe Church

語らい①（大江教会）　Talking with Parishioners ①（Oe Church）

語らい②（﨑津教会）　Talking with Parishioners ②（Sakitsu Church）

伴奏（﨑津教会）　Playing the Organ（Sakitsu Church）

ミサ（大江教会）　Mass（Oe Church）

被昇天祭
The Assumption

被昇天祭(8月15日)には、聖母マリアが天国に昇天されたことを記念する
The Assumption of Mary into heaven is celebrated on August 15th.

侍者　Altar Girl

花撒きの少女たち　Flower Bearers

行列　Procession

崎津みなとのフェスティバル
Sakitsu Summer Festival

夏のフェスティバルでは教会の上に花火があがる
Summer Fireworks Display in Sakitsu.

殉教祭
Martyrs' Festival

殉教祭はカトリック、仏式、神道合同で行われる天草を代表する祭礼だったが、今は中断されている
Martyrs' Festival, once celebrated by Catholics, Buddhists and Shintoists, is no longer held.

カトリック式典　Catholic Ceremony

仏式式典　Buddhist Ceremony

大江冬まつり
Oe Winter Festival

冬まつりはクリスマス イヴに大江教会を中心に行われる
This festival is held on Christmas Eve at Oe Church and nearby.

イルミネーション①　Christmas Lights ①

イルミネーション②　Christmas Lights ②

サンタクロースも参加　Santas Join in the Procession

キリスト教伝来450年記念祭
450th Anniversary Ceremony

キリスト教の天草伝来450年祭が2016年6月に開かれた
Celebration of the 450th Anniversary of Christianity in Amakusa held in June 2016.

宮原司教による記念ミサ（大江教会）　Mass by Bishop Miyahara（Oe Church）

© Carl Jenson　平和のための集会（﨑津教会）
Meeting for Peace（Sakitsu Church）

栄光の賛歌（大江教会）Singing Hymns（Oe Church）

祈り①　Offering Prayers ①

ミサ①　Mass ①

ミサ②　Mass ②

祈り②　Offering Prayers ②

© Carl Jenson　　　　　　　　　平和祈願の舞い（﨑津教会）　Praying for Peace through Shinto Dance（Sakitsu Church）

対話（左から田口宮司、池田住職、渡辺神父・﨑津教会）
Meeting for Peace（Sakitsu Church）
From the Left: Shinto Priest Taguchi,
Buddhist Priest Ikeda, Father Watanabe

祈り（池田住職・﨑津教会）
Priest Ikeda Offering Buddhist Prayers（Sakitsu Church）

| ハルブ神父 / Father Halbout | 1864年フランス生まれ。明治22年（1889）来日。昭和2年（1927）63才で﨑津教会に赴任。昭和9年（1934）現在の﨑津教会を建立。昭和20年（1945）﨑津で帰天。81才 | Born in France in 1864, he came to Japan in 1889, and to Sakitsu in 1927. He built Sakitsu Church in 1934. He died in Sakitsu in 1945 at age 81. |

オーグスチン ハルブ神父
Father August Halbout

墓碑（﨑津修道院前）
Grave (In Front of Sakitsu Convent)

| ガルニエ神父 / Father Garnier | 1860年フランス生まれ。明治18年（1885）来日。明治25年（1892）天草に赴任し、昭和17年（1942）天草で82才の生涯を終える。昭和8年（1933）現在の大江教会を建立 | Born in France in 1860, he came to Japan in 1885, and seven years later came to Amakusa. He died in Amakusa in 1942 at age 82. He built the present Oe Church in 1933. |

ルイ ガルニエ神父
Father Louis Garnier

墓碑（大江教会内）
Grave (At Oe Church)

| フェリエ神父 / Father Ferrier | 明治15年（1882）天草に赴任し2代目の大江教会を建立。明治20年（1887）今富の山中に孤児院「根引の子部屋」を創設した | He came to Amakusa in 1882 and rebuilt the Oe Church. He established an orphanage *Nebiki no Kobeya* in Imatomi in 1887. |

ジョセフ フェリエ神父像
Statue of Father Ferrier

アダム荒川 / Adam Arakawa

1552年島原生まれ。教会の看坊を務めながら深く信仰した。重なる拷問に耐えて棄教しなかったため1614年斬首された。2007年ローマ教皇はアダム荒川を「福者」に列福した

Born in Shimabara in 1552, he was a very devout Christian working for the Church.
He would not give up his Christian faith in spite of hard persecution, thus he was executed.
The Pope gave him beatification in 2007.

アダム荒川
Adam Arakawa

殉教400年祭　ⒸⒸ大江教会
400th Anniversary of martyrdom (Tomioka Castle)

アルメイダ / Almeida

1525年ポルトガル生まれ。1552年来日し1583年天草の河内浦で生涯を終えた。宣教師として布教活動を行いながら南蛮医としても活動した。1569年最初の﨑津教会を建立した

Born in Portugal in 1525, he came to Japan in 1552 and died in Kawachiura in Amakusa. He was a missionary and also worked as a doctor. He built the first Sakitsu Church in 1569.

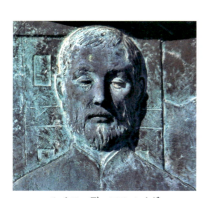

ルイス　デ　アルメイダ
Luis de Almeida

アルメイダ上陸地（河浦町）
Place of Arrival in Kawaura

天草四郎 / Shiro Amakusa

1623年生まれ。若くして天草・島原の乱（一揆）の総大将になる。1638年島原の原城でクリスチャンを含む一揆軍37000人とともに戦死する。不明な部分が多い

Born in 1623, he became the leader of the Amakusa-Shimabara Rebellion. He and 37,000 people including Christians were killed at Hara Castle in Shimabara in 1638. Many historical details remain unknown.

天草四郎像
Statue of Shiro Amakusa

天草四郎像（鬼池港）
Statue of Shiro Amakusa (Oniike Port)

弾圧 Persecution

キリシタンは厳しい弾圧でも信仰を守り抜いた
Christians kept their belief under hard persecution.

ⓒ 天草キリシタン館　　　　　　　　　　　　　　　高札　Bulletin Board

ⓒ 天草キリシタン館　　　絵踏み　*Efumi*　　ⓒ 天草キリシタン館　　踏み絵　*Fumie*

ⓒ 時事通信社
「日本キリシタン殉教史」

拷問（アダム荒川）　Torture (Adam Arakawa)

潜伏 Hiding

大江に残る隠れキリシタンの祈りの部屋。1814 年築
This is a hidden room that was built in 1814 in Oe.

隠れ部屋　Hidden Room

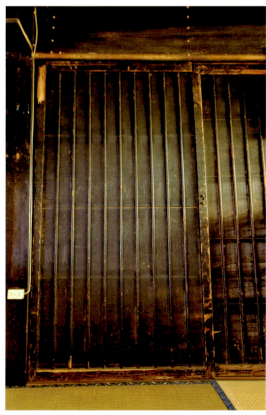

普段　Usual Appearance

開けて二階へ　Opened door leading upstairs

ⓒ 天草キリシタン館

ⓒ サンタマリア館

隠し十字仏　Cross Hidden inside Buddhist Statue

殿様像の背中に十字架
Cross on Back of Feudal Lord Statue

ⓒ 天草キリシタン館

ⓒ 﨑津教会資料館

マリア像代用の土人形　Clay Doll Regarded as Mary

柱の中の隠しメダイ　Faith Medal Hidden inside Pillar

天草の思いを世界へ

崎津教会・大江教会・本渡教会主任司祭　渡辺隆義

　ルイス・デ・アルメイダをはじめ宣教師たちが蒔いたキリスト教信仰の種は天草のあちこちで芽を出し、瞬く間に華を咲かせました。天草の土壌はキリスト教の発展のために適したもので、それは多くの宣教師たちが見抜いたように人々の知識欲と優れた倫理観によるものでもありました。このように順風満帆に見えた天草での布教（宣教）活動はやがて試練の時を迎えることになります。豊臣秀吉によるキリシタンへの弾圧政策は、徳川幕府に引き継がれてさらに激しさを増し、天草でも殉教者を出しました。1614年（慶長19）に苓北町で殉教したアダム荒川は現在も天草のキリスト信者の中で生き続けています。絵踏みによるキリシタン摘発の制度は潜伏キリシタンを生みました。キリストやマリアの絵を踏まされた人たちの心の痛みは計り知れないものがあります。また、宣教師追放がもたらした悲劇の一つは、キリスト教信仰の内容と実践の変容であり、このためにある人たちはアルメイダが伝えた信仰への復帰が困難になってしまいました。

　明治になって、キリスト教は天草でも復興の時代に入ります。長崎からやってきた信者に呼応して天草町や河浦町ではたくさんの人が洗礼を受けました。昭和の初期に信徒たちの祈りと労苦によって大江と崎津に建立された教会（天主堂）は今も天草の信仰のシンボルとして輝きを放っています。

大江教会　川上 謙二　Oe Church　Kenji Kawakami

教会の見える漁村風景　川上 謙二
View of Church in Fishing Village　Kenji Kawakami

　「キリスト教天草伝来450年祭」を実施することになり、福者アダム荒川の殉教記念日である2016年6月5日とその前日が開催日として選ばれました。苓北町にある天草中央キリスト教会では、アダム荒川の信仰について南圭生牧師が話してくださいました。アダム荒川が教派を超えたキリスト信者の交流のきっかけを作ってくれたものと感慨深いものがあります。アルメイダ終焉の地として知られる河浦町では、崎津教会に信福寺の池田集恵住職、鈴木神社の田口孝雄宮司をお招きして、それぞれの立場から天草におけるキリスト教を語っていただき、共に「平和のための祈り」を捧げました。このような日が来ることを誰か予見できたでしょうか。天草のキリスト教復興の地である天草町の大江教会では信者たちが自分たちの信仰の原点を再確認し、本渡では地域社会の人々と共に生きる教会を体現できました。
　かつて天草のキリスト教と仏教・神道の間にあった軋轢という不幸な歴史を今の時代の尺度で裁くことはできません。むしろ、ザビエルやアルメイダがそうであったように、私たちは、宗教、文化の違いを尊重し合い、互いのよいものを分かち合うなど、相互理解と平和への一歩を踏み出す必要があります。天草の思いがさざ波となって世界に広がっていきますように。

From Amakusa to the World

Luis de Almeida and other missionaries long ago sowed seeds of Christian faith. Those seeds sprouted buds all over Amakusa, and in the blink of eye had bloomed. The Amakusan soil was just right for Christianity to develop. The missionaries saw clearly the people's thirst for knowledge and high standards of morality. All was going very well for the missions but they would soon be put to the test. Toyotomi Hideyoshi issued a ban on Christianity. The situation intensified when the Tokugawa Shogunate took over and many were martyred. In 1614 Adam Arakawa was martyred in Reihoku but he lives on through the Christians in Amakusa. The practice of *efumi* used to detect Christians caused them to go underground. Those who were made to tread upon images of Jesus or Mary felt incredible pain in their hearts. The banishment of the missionaries led to a tragedy in which Christian faith changed in content and form. A discord in faith was brought about; over time their faith had drifted and many found it difficult to return to the teachings of Almeida.

The Meiji era brought in a restoration of Christianity in Amakusa. Christians from Nagasaki came to Amakusa Town and Kawaura to teach the Christian faith resulting in many baptisms. At the beginning of the Showa era the Oe and Sakitsu Churches were built as a testament to the prayers and hardships of Christians in Amakusa, and stand as shining symbols of their faith.

The celebration of the 450th Anniversary of Christianity in Amakusa was held on June 5th 2016—the memorial day of the martyrdom of Adam Arakawa—as well as the day before. Pastor Keisei Minami talked about the faith of Adam Arakawa at the Amakusa Chuo Christian Church. I feel strongly that Adam Arakawa has transcended his own religious denomination to bring us an occasion for interfaith communication. Kawaura is known as the town in which Almeida lived out his final days. And here in this town at the Sakitsu Church, Buddhist chief priest Shue Ikeda and Shinto chief priest Takao Taguchi were invited to speak about their views on Christianity in Amakusa, and to offer "prayers for peace." At the Oe Church that once experienced a revival, Christians reconfirmed their faith. The Hondo Catholic Church embodies a community of believers that lives in harmony with the local community.

In the past there has been a sad history of conflict between Christianity and Buddhism as well as Shintoism. However, we can no longer regard each other with those old feelings of antipathy. As it was with Xavier and Almeida, we must respect our cultural and religious differences in order to move forward in mutual understanding toward a peaceful coexistence. May this ripple in the sea of Amakusa spread throughout the world.

Father Takayoshi Watanabe

天草中央キリスト教会にて、右から
レオ神父
南牧師
宮原司教
筆者
From the right:
Father Leo
Pastor Minami
Bishop Miyahara
Father Watanabe

天草のキリスト教史

天草市 世界遺産推進室 元室長 平田豊弘

はじめに

　天草のキリスト教は、16世紀後半の伝来と繁栄、江戸時代の禁教政策での弾圧と潜伏キリシタンとしての信仰継承、明治時代の禁教令撤廃による再布教と復活、という歴史を刻んでいます。特に、江戸時代の禁教期における200年余りにおよぶ潜伏キリシタンの存在は、世界の宗教史の上で特筆すべき出来事です。

①伝来と展開

　1543年、鹿児島県の種子島に鉄砲が伝来し、戦国時代の日本に大きな変化をもたらします。そして、1549年にはフランシスコ・ザビエル（Fig. 1）によってキリスト教の布教が開始されました。各地の大名は、南蛮船の来航を求め、鉄砲などの南蛮貿易と引き替えにキリスト教を受け入れます。この頃の天草は、大矢野氏、上津浦氏、栖本氏、志岐氏、天草氏の5人の領主（天草五人衆）により支配されていました（Fig. 2）。特に志岐鎮経は、キリシタン大名大村純忠の弟である諸経を養子としました。志岐氏の要請により、1566年アルメイダ修道士により天草での布教が始まります。志岐には教会堂が建てられ、多くの神父が来島しました。1568年と1570年には全国の宣教師会議が開催されたことは、キリスト教布教にとって天草が重要地であったことが伺えます。しかし、鎮経は期待した南蛮貿易が進まないため棄教を宣言し、布教の中心は天草鎮尚の領地である河内浦に移りました。天草氏領での宣教活動は進展し、30余りの教会が建てられ信者は1万5千人以上に達します。その後大矢野氏、栖本氏そして上津浦氏と天草五人衆は順次入信していきました。

Fig. 1　Francis Xavier

Fig. 2　Map of *Amakusa Goninshu*

②小西行長の天草支配と天草コレジヨ

　1587年、豊臣秀吉により伴天連追放令が出されました。これは、外国人宣教師、修道士の国外退去、布教禁止などを盛り込んだものでしたが、貿易は容認しており取り締まりは徹底されていません。このため、宣教師は密かに布教活動を続けることになります。1589年、天正の天草合戦後、天草は小西行長領になります。キリシタン大名である行長はキリスト教を擁護し、1591年には島原の加津佐にあったコレジヨが天草に移されました。コレジヨは宣教師を養成する大神学校で、ラテン語、ポルトガル語、日本語の三か国語が必修であり、哲学、倫理学、文学、音楽などが教えられていました。ここには、イエズス会によりヨーロッパに派遣されローマ教皇に謁見した4少年（伊東マンショ、千々石ミゲル、中浦ジュリアン、原マルティノ）も入校しています（Fig. 3）。4人の少年使節はさまざまなものを持ち帰りましたが、日本の文化に多大な影響を与えたのがグーテンベルク印刷機です。天草では『平家物語』、『イソップ物語』などのローマ字本や『どちりな・きりしたん』などの教義書が印刷されました。

4人の遣欧少年使節
Fig. 3　Mission of 4 Boys

③寺沢氏の天草支配と島原・天草一揆

　1600年、関ヶ原の戦いで小西行長が敗れた後、天草は肥前唐津城主の寺沢広高の領地になります。国内のキリシタン弾圧が強まるとともに、広高は次第に取締りを強めていきます。二代寺沢堅高が支配するようになると、弾圧はさらに厳しくなりました。1634年以降、天草・島原地方では天候不順による飢饉が続きました。しかし、領主の年貢の取り立ては厳しく、これまでのキリシタン弾圧と重なり農民の不満が蓄積し爆発します。1637年10月、島原半島で農民一揆が起こり、これに呼応して天草の農民も立ち上がりました。一揆軍は16歳の天草四郎を総大将に、12月に南有馬の原城に籠城します。一揆軍3万7千人に対し、幕府軍12万5千人は原城を包囲し、兵糧攻めにします。ついに1638年2月28日、一揆軍は全滅し終結しました。これが「島原・天草一揆」で、成立間もない江戸幕府を震撼させる出来事となり、この後、日本は鎖国体制をとることになりました。

鈴木三公
Fig. 4　3 Figures of the Suzuki Clan

④天領天草と天草崩れ

　島原・天草一揆のあと、天草は山崎家治領を経て1641年に江戸幕府が治める天領となり、鈴木重成が代官として着任します。重成は兄の鈴木正三の協力も得て、寺院・神社の再建や移民政策など天草の復興に尽力しました。さらに後任の鈴木重辰（正三の子、重成の養子）も行政改革を行い天草の振興に努めます（Fig. 4）。1644年、天草は戸田忠昌領となり、1671年には再び天領として、明治時代まで続きます。1805年、崎津村、今富村、大江村、高浜村で多くの潜伏キリシタンが発覚する「天草崩れ」と呼ばれる事件が起きました。代官所の取調べで5205人もの信者が発覚します。この事件によって禁教下における信仰の組織や形態の詳細が明らかになりました（Fig. 5）。

古文書
Fig. 5　Old Documents

⑤キリスト教の解禁と復活

　1865年、長崎にフランス人のキリスト教徒のため大浦天主堂が建立されました。ここを浦上の潜伏キリシタンが訪れ、キリシタン信者であることを告白しました。このことは「信徒発見」として海外に宗教史上の奇跡と伝えられます。そして1873年、明治政府はキリシタン禁令の高札を撤去し、キリスト教を黙認することになりました。黙認により天草には長崎から宣教師が派遣され、潜伏キリシタンは教会へ復帰するか、隠れキリシタンとして信仰するかの道を辿ります。大江村、崎津村は教会に復帰しますが、今富村は「水方」と呼ばれる有力な指導者がいたため隠れキリシタンとしての信仰が1940年代まで続きます。

　1885年、大江教会が建てられ、翌年には崎津教会が建てられました。現在の大江教会は、ガルニエ神父と信者たちが私財や労力を投じて1933年完成させたものです。崎津教会は、ハルブ神父が1934年に完成させたものです。両教会を手掛けたのは、多くの教会を建築した長崎の鉄川与助でした（Fig. 6）。

鉄川与助
Fig. 6　Yosuke Tetsukawa

Amakusa's Christian History

Toyohiro Hirata

Former Director, World Heritage Promotion Center, Amakusa City

Preface

Christianity was introduced and began to flourish in Amakusa in the second half of the 16th century. Although a ban on Christianity went into effect during the Edo Period (1603—1868), a number of believers continued to practice covertly as 'Hidden Christians'. When the ban was finally lifted in the Meiji Period (1868—1912), Christianity experienced a revival. This history, and especially the perseverance of Hidden Christians spanning more than 200 years of prohibition during the Edo Period, is significant enough to be recorded in the annals of world religion.

① Introduction and Development

In 1543, firearms were introduced to Japan at Tanegashima Island in today's Kagoshima Prefecture. This had a profound effect on the country, which was in the throes of civil war at the time. Subsequently in 1549, the missionary Francis Xavier began to propagate Christianity in the same area (Fig. 1). Feudal lords in various parts of Japan sought to engage in firearm trade with foreign ships and in so doing, they also came into contact with Christian religion. Around this time, Amakusa was ruled by five powerful clans: Oyano, Kotsuura, Sumoto, Shiki, and Amakusa (Fig. 2). In particular, Shigetsune Shiki adopted as his son Morotsune Shiki, who was the younger brother of Sumitada Omura, a prominent Christian lord in nearby Nagasaki. In 1566, on the request of Shiki, a Jesuit missionary named Luis de Almeida began to disseminate Christianity in Amakusa. A church was built in Shiki village, and many priests came to Amakusa. Particularly in the years 1568 and 1570, when missionaries from all over Japan attended conventions in Amakusa became a significant place for the nation-wide propagation of Christianity. However, when the trade with foreigners that Shigetsune envisioned did not materialize, he renounced his Christian faith. This in turn resulted in the center of missionary activity moving south to Kawachiura, an area under the jurisdiction of Shigehisa Amakusa.

Missionary work in Amakusa continued, resulting in about 30 churches being built, and the number of followers exceeding 15,000. In time, the remaining three local rulers, Oyano, Sumoto, and Kotsuura also converted to Christianity.

② The reign of Yukinaga Konishi and the Amakusa Colegio

In 1587, Japan's supreme leader Hideyoshi Toyotomi issued the Purge Directive to the Jesuits, and Christian missionaries and monks were ordered to stop proselytizing. However, since trade with foreigners was allowed, the order could not be effectively enforced, and missionaries continued their work in a clandestine fashion.

In 1589, after the Tensho Conflict, Amakusa became the demesne of Yukinaga Konishi. Yukinaga was a Christian sympathizer, and in 1591 he relocated a seminary known as 'Colegio' from Kazusa on the Shimabara Peninsula to Amakusa. Missionaries in training here took compulsory courses in Latin, Portuguese, and Japanese. Philosophy, Ethics, Literature and Music were also taught. The four boys (Mancio Ito, Miguel Chijiwa, Juliao Nakaura, Martinho Hara) that were dispatched to Rome by the Jesuits for an audience with the Pope also enrolled and studied here in order to attain priesthood (Fig. 3).

When these four boys returned from their diplomatic mission, they brought back with them various things. Most noteworthy of these was a Gutenberg Press, which proved to have much influence on Japanese culture. It was used to print the Japanese Legend 'Heike Monogatari' as well as 'Aesop's Fables' in Japanese but using the Latin alphabet. 'Dochirina Kirishitan', a book on Christian doctrine, was also among the books printed.

③ The reign of Terasawa and the Shimabara-amakusa rebellion

In 1600, after the defeat of Yukinaga Konishi at the Battle of Sekigahara, Amakusa fell under the control of Karatsu Castle in Hizen province and its ruler Hirotaka Terasawa. As oppression of Christians spread through Japan, Hirotaka began enforcing a policy of strict control. His successor Katataka Terasawa continued a reign of unyielding oppression.

In 1634, a period of unfavorable climate began affecting the Shimabara and Amakusa districts, resulting in famine. In October 1637, a peasant uprising erupted in the Shimabara Peninsula, and Amakusa peasants soon followed suit. Sixteen-year-old Shiro Amakusa became the leader of the rebellion. After some initial successes, the rebels were eventually forced to hole up at Hara Castle in Minami-Arima. In all, the rebels numbered 37,000 while the shogunate's 125,000-strong army lay siege to the castle in order to starve out its occupants. On February 28th, 1638, amid constant attacks, the rebels unanimously decided to fight the losing battle to the death, and a massacre followed. Although victorious, this Shimabara-Amakusa Rebellion shook the newly-formed Tokugawa Shogunate enough to subsequently implement a policy of total seclusion of Japan.

④ **Shogunate control and '*Amakusa Kuzure*'**

After the Shimabara-Amakusa Rebellion, the shogunate handed the Amakusa islands to Icharu Yamazaki. Then in 1641, Amakusa came to be under direct control of the shogunate, and Shigenari Suzuki took up the new post of appointed governor. He dedicated himself to the revival of the region devastated by the rebellion. With the help of his elder brother, Shosan Suzuki, he rebuilt temples and shrines in all areas of the islands, and issued a forced immigration order to replenish the population. His successor Shigetoki Suzuki (Shosan's child, Shigenari's adopted son) continued Shigenari's efforts and performed administrative reforms (Fig. 4). In 1664, Amakusa fell under the reign of Tadamasa Toda but in 1671 imperial reign was once again re-established, to continue for the next 197 years until the Meiji Restoration.

In 1805, it was discovered that many 'hidden' Christians existed in parts of Amakusa's Sakitsu, Imatomi, Oe, and Takahama villages, leading to the so-called '*Amakusa Kuzure*' (Amakusa Debacle) incident. The magistrate's office conducted an investigation, 5,205 practioners were indeed identified, and their confessions were recorded. According to extant archives, a number of religious organizations, festivals, prayers, devotional objects, and sacred places were also uncovered (Fig. 5).

⑤ **Ban on Christianity lifted, Revival**

In 1865, the Oura Catholic Church was built in Nagasaki for the benefit of French Christians living there. When some hidden Christians from Urakami in Nagasaki visited the church, they confessed their Christian faith. In historical records outside Japan, this 'discovery of believers' was reported as nothing less than a miracle. In 1873, the Meiji government finally not only lifted the ban on Christianity in Japan, but gave Christianity a tacit approval. At this time missionaries from Nagasaki were dispatched to Amakusa, where hidden Christians faced a dilemma of whether to come out of hiding and join a church, or continue their religious practices covertly. Oe and Sakitsu villagers returned to their churches. However, Imatomi village's religious leaders, referred to as *mizukata*, continued to be active, and the villagers maintained their clandestine form of worship until finally coming out of hiding in the 1940s.

In 1885, the Oe Church was built, and the following year saw the building of Sakitsu Church. Father Garnier oversaw the building of the present-day Oe Church; funds and labor were both provided by the devotees, and it was completed in 1933. Sakitsu Church was completed by Father Halbout in 1934. Yosuke Tetsukawa, well known for the construction of numerous other churches, was responsible for the construction of both Oe and Sakitsu (Fig. 6).

Graced by their churches, the scenic villages of Oe and Sakitsu, with their 400 years of Christian history, are a precious part of Amakusa's cultural heritage.

世界遺産の﨑津集落

天草市 世界遺産推進室 元室長 平田豊弘

はじめに

天草の﨑津集落は、禁教期において仏教、神道、キリスト教が共存し、漁村特有の信仰形態を育んだ集落です。「長崎と天草地方の潜伏キリシタン関連遺産」として、長崎県の11の資産とともに2018年（平成30年）の世界遺産に登録されました。

﨑津集落の概要

1566年、イエズス会修道士アルメイダにより志岐にキリスト教が伝来し、﨑津では1569年に宣教が開始され、殆どの村人がキリスト教徒となりました。ルイス・フロイスの「日本史」には、﨑津は「さしのつ」と呼ばれ、布教拠点として重要視されていたことが記され、それを裏付けるように伝来期のメダイやロザリオが現存しています。集落内には教会堂や宣教師のレジデンシアが作られ、教会を支援する信仰組織として3つの小組からなるコンフラリアが形成されました。

1589年の天正の天草合戦の後、天草はキリシタン大名である小西行長が支配し、天草のキリスト教は全盛を迎えます（Fig. 7）。特に1591年から1597年の間、宣教師を養成するコレジヨが天草氏の居城のある河内浦に設置されました。ここには天正遣欧少年使節団の4人（伊東マンショ、千々石ミゲル、中浦ジュリアン、原マルティノ）も入校し、彼らが持ち帰ったグーテンベルク印刷機により、ローマ字活版印刷が行われました。このコレジヨの印刷事業を支えた村の一つが、﨑津集落のコンフラリアと推測されます（Fig. 8）。﨑津では、白蝶貝で作られた聖イグナチオ・ロヨラのメダイが3個発見されていますが、これには印刷所で本の表紙を作るエッチング技法が活かされているのです。1614年、江戸幕府が禁教令を発布し、信徒への迫害が強まるなか、﨑津集落には多くの潜伏キリシタンがいました。1617年にイエズス会が作成した「コウロス徴収文書」には、天草のコンフラリア組織と59名の署名・捺印があります。ここには﨑津の信仰組織の代表者3名の名前と洗礼名が記載されており、宣教師が密かに来訪し「こんひさん（告解）」や「貴きさからめんと（聖体の秘蹟）」を授けていたことが判明しています（Fig. 9）。

禁教令により宣教師は追放され、1637年、厳しい弾圧、苛政や飢饉を契機として、島原・天草一揆が勃発しました。天草での一揆は大矢野から始まり、本渡での激戦を経て富岡城での攻防戦となります。島原半島に面した大矢野、上津浦、二江、坂瀬川ではコンフラリアを母体に一揆に参加したと思われます。12月、島原と天草の一揆軍は原城に籠城しますが、翌年2月28日の総攻撃を受け全滅します。高浜、大江、今富、﨑津の村々は一揆に参加していないため、一揆終結後もコンフラリアの小組が継続し、潜伏キリシタンとしての信仰を支える組織になりました。幕府の宗教政策により、村人は表向きは神社の氏子になり寺院の門徒として生活しますが、密かにキリスト教の信仰を継続したのです。

小西行長
Fig. 7 Yukinaga Konishi

﨑津古地図
Fig. 8 Old Map of Sakitsu

布教当時の十字架
Fig. 9 Old Cross

天草では毎年3月頃、庄屋役宅で「絵踏み」が行われました。村人は役人の前で、キリストや聖母マリアの像を踏まされました。﨑津・今富・大江の人々は家に帰ると教義書「こんちりさんのりやく」を唱え、神の許しを得ています。﨑津では宣教師不在のなかでも、「水方」と呼ばれる信仰指導者が洗礼を授け、葬送儀礼や日繰りをもとに祭礼を行っています。また、「宿老」と呼ばれる組織指導者などが組織を支え、密かに信仰を継承する重要な役目を果たしました。﨑津集落には水方を勤めた家が現在も残り、潜伏時代の信心具などが保存されてます。

白蝶貝のメダイ
Fig. 10 "Medal" of White Lipped Oyster

　特に漁村である﨑津では、デウスを豊漁の神として崇拝しています。また、アワビやタイラギの貝殻の内側の模様を、聖母マリアに見立てて崇敬するなど漁村特有の信仰形態が形成されました（Fig. 10）、（Fig. 12）。仏教行事である盆には仏壇や祭壇に魚肉を供え、オラショを唱えていました（Fig. 11）。さらに村人が寺院や神社に参詣するときは「あんめんりゆす＝アーメンデウス」と唱え、神道、仏教、潜伏キリシタンの宗教間の共存が図られていたことも判明しています。

オラショ
Fig. 11　Prayer Scrolls

　1805年、﨑津や近隣の3村では、潜伏キリシタンが発覚する「天草崩れ」が起こります。その発端はクリスマス近くになると牛を殺し、その肉を仏壇に供えているという風習や仏像と異なる像を信仰していることが露見したためです。この事件での異教徒は5205名ですが、﨑津では村人2401名のうち1709名（71％）が信徒として検挙され、自白書が作成されました。こうした古文書により、禁教期の信仰組織や信仰形態が明らかになっています。

　1873年、キリシタン禁教令が撤廃されると長崎の西政吉が大江を訪れ天草での復活を呼びかけます。1877年、巡回宣教師としてマルマン神父が来島し、次のコール神父は潜伏キリシタンの子孫

マリアに見立てたアワビ
Fig. 12　Abalone Shell as Mary

の発見に力を注ぎました。1880年、ボンヌ神父は大江に定住して宣教し、﨑津、今富、大江での信徒数は375名を数えました。3村の教会への復帰については、1882年頃にフェリエ神父が大江と﨑津での調査が伝えています。1934年、ハルブ神父の希望により禁教期に絵踏みをしていた吉田庄屋役宅跡を購入し、﨑津教会が建設されました。今の祭壇は、まさに絵踏みが行われた場所に位置しているのです。﨑津集落の中で高くそびえる教会の尖塔は、この地に刻まれた450年の歴史と文化、人々の営みの象徴と言えるでしょう。

世界遺産の﨑津集落

　世界遺産に登録された「天草の﨑津集落」の資産の範囲は、16世紀の教会推定地や禁教期に潜伏キリシタンが崇敬するとともに、「天草崩れ」での取締りの舞台となった﨑津諏訪神社、信仰指導者である「水方」の家、絵踏みが行われた﨑津吉田庄屋役宅跡（現在の﨑津教会）などを中心に、これらとかかわりが深い信仰形態を示す範囲が設定されています。

　﨑津集落は、禁教期においても潜伏キリシタンとして漁村特有の信仰形態が続けられていたことなど、その資産価値は世界的にも重要です。

World Heritage Status of Sakitsu Village

Toyohiro Hirata

Former Director, World Heritage Promotion Center, Amakusa City

Preface

Sakitsu is a fishing village in Amakusa where during times of religious prohibition, a unique combination of Buddhist, Shinto, and Christian faiths developed. Sakitsu has achieved a World Heritage Site in 2018, alongside 11 sites in Nagasaki Prefecture, which are to be registered as 'Hidden Christian Sites in the Nagasaki Region'.

About Sakitsu Village

In 1566 a Jesuit missionary named Luis de Almeida introduced Christianity to Shiki and in 1569, he began a mission in Sakitsu, managing to convert virtually all the villagers there. In Luis Frois's *History of Japan*, Sakitsu was referred to as '*Sashinotsu*' and was regarded as an important missionary base; this is substantiated by extant medallions and rosaries. A chapel and missionary quarters (*residencia*) were constructed and these were supported by a religious organization (*confraria* or fraternity) composed in turn of three smaller groups of believers.

In 1589, after the Tensho conflict, Amakusa came under the jurisdiction of Christian feudal lord Yukinaga Konishi and Christianity in Amakusa reached its golden age (Fig. 7). Notably, between 1591 and 1597, a seminary called *Colegio* was active in Kawachiura, where the castle of the Amakusa clan was also located. This is where the four boys comprising the Tensho Embassy to Europe had studied. When they returned, they brought with them a Gutenberg Press, which was used to print books using the Latin alphabet for the first time in Japan. It is thought that the *confraria* of Sakitsu village was one of the organizations that supported the printing operations (Fig. 8). In Sakitsu, three medallions made from pearl oyster shells with images of St. Ignacio de Loyola were discovered. They were made using an etching technique normally used to decorate the front covers of books. In 1614, the Edo shogunate issued an order prohibiting religion, and as persecution became the norm, many Sakitsu Christians began to conceal their faith. The 1617 Couros Tax Assessment Document, compiled by the Jesuits, contains the names and seals of 59 members of the Amakusa *confraria*. Among these are the Japanese names and Christian baptismal names of three representatives from Sakitsu. The record shows that they were visited in secret by a priest who received their confessions and administered the Holy Sacrament to them (Fig. 9).

The Edo prohibition order banished missionaries from Japan, and the increasing oppression and tyranny, as well as famine, led in 1637 to the Shimabara-Amakusa Rebellion. In Amakusa, the rebellion began at Oyano, continued with a fierce battle in Hondo, and culminated with an attack on Tomioka Castle. The *confrarias* of Oyano, Kotsuura, Futae, and Sakasegawa formed the core of the Amakusa rebels. In December these and the Shimabara rebels were forced to hole up at Hara Castle only to be completely annihilated on February 28th of the following year. The villages of Takahama, Oe, Imatomi, and Sakitsu did not participate in the rebellion, and after its conclusion, small groups comprising the *confraria* continued to be active, supporting covert believers. As per the shogunate's policy on religion, villagers maintained outward appearances by visiting Shinto shrines or Buddhist temples, while clandestinely continuing their Christian practices.

In Amakusa, around March of every year, the *efumi* ritual was carried out at the residence (*shoya*) of each village headman. Watched by an official, every villager had to tread on an image of Christ or the Virgin Mary. Sakitsu, Imatomi, and Oe villagers, upon returning home, would recite the prayer '*konchirisan-no-riyaku*', asking for God's forgiveness. Although there was no missionary in residence at Sakitsu, there was a designated religious leader called *mizukata*; he would administer baptisms, funeral rites, and preside over other ceremonies according to the religious calendar. So-called *shukuro* (elders), were instrumental in maintaining and propagating the clandestine organization. A *mizukata* residence is still extant in the village, as are various religious artifacts from the hidden Christian period.

Peculiar religious practices emerged, especially in the fishing village of Sakitsu. "Deus" was worshipped as a god who would ensure a plentiful catch of fish. Also, mother-of-pearl patterns on the inner surfaces of abalone and fan mussel shells were likened to Virgin Mary and revered (Fig. 10, Fig. 12). Fish meat was put into bowls normally used for Buddhist ceremonies and placed on the household altars as an offering, while prayers were chanted (Fig. 11). When villagers visited a shrine or temple, they would chant *anmenriyusu* (Amen Deus). It can be said that the villagers created a melange of Buddhism, Shinto, and Christianity in order to protect and maintain their culture and customs.

In 1805, hidden Christians were exposed in Sakitsu and its three neighboring villages, and the *Amakusa Kuzure*, or 'Amakusa Debacle' incident followed. Suspicions initially arose when it was found that around Christmas time the villagers would slaughter a cow and place the meat on their household altars as an offering. It was also noticed that they worshipped idols that differed from the usual Buddhist images. An investigation followed, and 5205 people were identified as believers. Out of 2,401 Sakitsu villagers, 1,709 (71%) were identified as followers; their confessions were recorded in writing. By referring to such historical records, the believer's organizations, practices, festivals, prayers, devotional objects, and sacred places can be identified.

In 1873 the prohibition of Christianity was lifted, and when Masakichi Nishi of Nagasaki visited Oe, he called for Amakusa's revival. In 1877, Father Marmand was installed in Amakusa, making rounds of the local churches. Father Corr, who followed him, made efforts to find descendants of hidden Christians among the local people. In 1880, Father Bonne settled permanently in Oe to continue missionary work. At this time, 375 followers were counted among the villagers of Sakitsu, Imatomi, and Oe. A type of parsley that grows wild in Oe and Sakitsu, locally referred to as *pateru-seri* or *bon-seri*, is in fact a parsley that Bonne himself introduced to Amakusa. An 1882 report by Father Ferrier talks about the residents of Oe and Sakitsu coming out of hiding and joining the church community. In 1934, the remains of Yoshida *shoya* where *efumi* rituals had taken place during the prohibition were purchased according to the wishes of Father Halbout, who also oversaw the building of Sakitsu church. The current altar in the church is placed at the very spot where *efumi* rituals had previously taken place. It can be said that the steeple of the church, towering above the surrounding houses, symbolizes 450 years of Christian history, culture and the local people's toils.

World Heritage Status of Sakitsu Village

We believe that the presumed location of the 16th century church, the plight of the hidden Christians who continued to worship throughout the prohibition of Christianity during the Edo period, the Sakitsu Suwa shrine which was the main stage of the events of the *'Amakusa Kuzure'* crackdown, the remains of the *'Mizukata'* (appointed religious leader's) residence, and the location of the Yoshida *shoya* where the *efumi* Christian renunciation ritual took place (in fact the present day location of the Sakitsu Church), together constitute a cultural resource worthy of the World Heritage title.

The inhabitants of the fishing village of Sakitsu continued their unique style of worship as hidden Christians during more than two centuries of religious prohibition. Sakitsu constitutes a unique cultural phenomenon worthy of worldwide recognition.

歴史地図　Historical Map

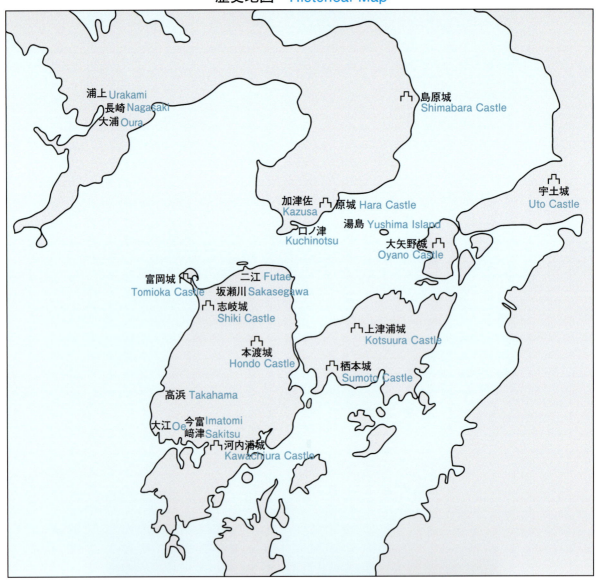

﨑津・大江周辺の衛星写真　Satellite Photo of Sakitsu, Oe

天草のキリスト教年表

	西暦（和暦）	天草の出来事	日本の出来事
宣教時代	1543（天文 12）		種子島に鉄砲伝来
	1549（天文 18）		ザビエルが鹿児島に上陸し布教開始
	1563（永禄 6）		大村純忠が最初のキリシタン大名となる
	1566（永禄 9）	アルメイダが志岐で布教開始	
	1568（永禄 11）	全国宣教師会議	
	1570（元亀元年）	全国宣教師会議（天草で2回目）	
	1582（天正 10）		少年遣欧使節のローマ派遣（～1590）
	1583（天正 11）	アルメイダが河内浦で帰天	
	1587（天正 15）		豊臣秀吉が伴天連追放令発布
	1588（天正 16）		小西行長が宇土城主になる
	1589（天正 17）	天正の天草合戦（天草五人衆敗北）	
	1591（天正 19）	コレジヨが河内浦に移る。天草本出版	
	1597（慶長元年）		二十六聖人が長崎の西坂で殉教
	1600（慶長 5）		関ヶ原の合戦。小西行長処刑
	1601（慶長 6）	天草が寺沢広高領となる	
弾圧・潜伏時代	1614（慶長 19）	アダム荒川の殉教	江戸幕府がキリスト教禁教令を出す
	1616（元和 2）		江戸幕府が再びキリスト教禁教令を出す
	1637（寛永 14）	島原・天草一揆起こる	
	1638（寛永 15）	原城落城。島原・天草一揆終結	
	1639（寛永 16）		鎖国令発布
	1641（寛永 18）	天草が天領となる	オランダ商館出島に移る
	1647（正保 4）	富岡吉利支丹供養碑建立	
	1654（承応 3）	切支丹禁制の高札が建つ	
	1804（文化元年）	潜伏キリシタン発覚	
	1805（文化 2）	天草崩れ	
	1853（嘉永 6）		ペリーが浦賀に来航
	1865（元治 2）	信徒発見	大浦天主堂建立
	1867（慶応 3）		大政奉還
復活時代	1873（明治 6）		切支丹禁令の高札撤去
	1874（明治 7）	大江に仮説教所設置	
	1883（明治 16）	フェリエ神父が大江に着任	
	1885（明治 18）	大江教会建立（1888年﨑津教会建立）	
	1889（明治 22）		大日本帝国憲法発布（条件付宗教の自由）
	1892（明治 25）	ガルニエ神父が大江教会に着任	
	1927（昭和 2）	ハルブ神父が﨑津教会に着任	
	1933（昭和 8）	現大江教会建立	
	1934（昭和 9）	現﨑津教会建立	
	1946（昭和 21）		日本国憲法発布（宗教の自由が明文化）
	1981（昭和 56）		ローマ教皇ヨハネ・パウロ2世来日
	2007（平成 19）	アダム荒川が福者に列福される	
	2016（平成 28）	天草キリスト教伝来450年記念式典	

Chronology of Amakusa's Christianity History

	Year	Historical Events in Amakusa	Historical Events In Japan
Missionary Period	1543		Guns introduced to Tanegashima Island
	1549		Francis Xavier arrived in Kagoshima and began propagation of Christianity
	1563		Sumitada Omura became the first Christian among feudal loads
	1566	Almeida began propagation of Christianity	
	1568	All Japan convention of missonaries	
	1570	All Japan convention of missonaries (2nd)	
	1582		Tensho Embassy Boys dispatched to Rome (returned in 1590)
	1583	Almeida died in Kawachiura, Amakusa	
	1587		Hideyoshi expelled Jesuit missionaries
	1588		Yukinaga Konishi became lord of Uto castle
	1589	Tensho Battle (five Amakusa lords defeated)	
	1591	Collegio moved to Kawachiura, Amakusa. *Amakusa Bon* books printed	
	1597		Martyrdom of 26 Martyrs in Nagasaki
	1600		Battle of Sekigahara. Yukinaga Konishi executed
	1601	Amakusa became a territory of Lord Hirotaka Terasawa	
Oppression and Hiding Period	1614	Adam Arakawa's matyrdom	Tokugawa Shogunate issued a proclamation banning Christianity
	1616		Tokugawa Shogunate reissued a proclamation banning Christianity
	1637	Shimabara-Amakusa Rebellion	
	1638	Hara castle destroyed. Shimabara-Amakusa Rebellion terminated	
	1639		First National Isolation Edict issued
	1641	Amakusa Shogun's demesne began	The Dutch trading house moved to Dejima
	1647	Christian memorial monument built in Tomioka	
	1654	Bulletin board banning Christianity displayed	
	1804	Hidden Christians discovered in Amakusa	
	1805	*Amakusa Kuzure* crackdown on Hidden Christians	
	1853		Perry visited Uraga
	1865	Discovery that Hidden Christians had survived	Oura church in Nagasaki City completed
	1867		Restoration of imperial rule
Restoration Period	1873		Bulletin board banning Christianity removed
	1874	Temporary preaching house was built in Oe	
	1883	Father Ferrier arrived in Oe	
	1885	Oe Church built	
	1889		Meiji Constitution issued and religious liberty allowed
	1892	Father Garnier arrived in Oe Church	
	1927	Father Halbout arrived in Sakitsu Church	
	1933	Current Oe Church rebuilt	
	1934	Current Sakitsu Church rebuilt	
	1946		The Constitution of Japan issued
	1981		Pope John Paul visited Japan
	2007	Adam Arakawa beatified	
	2016	Celebration of the 450th Anniversary of Christianty in Amakusa	

資料館の案内

天草キリシタン館　元館長 亀子研二

天草キリシタン館
Amakusa Christian Museum

43〜45ページも参照

フロイスの日本史に登場する天正の天草合戦の舞台になった本渡城趾に、天草キリシタン館はあります。

通称「殉教公園」と呼ばれているこの丘には天草・島原の一揆（乱）の戦没者を祀る殉教戦千人塚やキリシタン墓地などがありパノラマ状に市街地を一望でき、散策も楽しめます。

館内は天草・島原の一揆を中心に、天草キリシタン史、南蛮文化の伝来、一揆後の天草復興とキリスト教信仰の4つのゾーンが設けられ、キリシタンの歴史が臨場感豊かにわかりやすく展示されています。1637年（寛永14）天草・島原の一揆で使用された天草四郎陣中旗（国指定重要文化財：綸子着色聖体秘蹟図指物）は必見です。屋外エスカレーター、車椅子専用リフト、館内エレベーターなど完備されています。

【問】Tel. 0969 − 22 − 3845
〒863-0017 天草市船之尾町19 − 52
【営】8：30〜18：00　【休】12/30〜1/1
【料】一般300円　高校生200円　小・中学生150円
20名以上の団体は2割引

前景　Front View

ロザリオと壺　Rosary and Pot

マリア像　Statue of Mary

Amakusa Christian Museum is located at the site of the Hondo Castle where the Tensho Battle was fought in 1589. On this hill now called *Junkyo Koen* (Martyrdom Park) are *Senninzuka* which honors people killed in the Amakusa-Shimabara Rebellion, and a Christian graveyard. We can take in a nice view of Hondo and enjoy a pleasant walk. There are 4 sections within the museum. With emphasis mainly on the Amakusa-Shimabara Rebellion, the other sections incude Christian history of Amakusa, Introduction of Western Culture and Reconstruction of Amakusa after the Rebellion and Christian Faith in Amakusa. We recommend you see the War Banner of Shiro Amakusa (leader of Amakusa) Shimabara Rebellion. This banner was used in the rebellion.

Open: 8:30~18:00 Closed: 12/31~1/1
Address: 19-52 Funenoo-machi Amakusa-shi Kumamoto-ken 863-0017
Phone: 0969-22-3845
HP: http://www.city.amakusa.kumamoto.jp/kirishitan/

天草コレジヨ館
Amakusa Colegio Museum

47ページも参照

天草にキリスト教を伝道したルイス・デ・アルメイダ修道士が上陸したといわれるところの近くに天草コレジヨ館はあります。コレジヨとは、カトリック司祭を養成するためにイエズス会が設置した教育機関（大神学校）のことです。

16世紀に天正少年遣欧使節達が持ち帰ったキリスト教文化はどこよりも早く天草で華開きました。天草コレジヨでは、当時のヨーロッパの最高水準の学問が講義され、併設の印刷所では多くの天草本が印刷されました。日本初の金属活字印刷によるローマ字本「伊曽保物語」や「平家物語」、グーテンベルク印刷機、南蛮屏風など（いずれも複製）を展示。古楽器（竹製のパイプオルガン・バージナルなど）の体験演奏や少年使節の足跡をたどる映像鑑賞などもできます。2階には世界平和大使人形の館もあります。

【問】Tel. 0969 - 76 - 0388
〒863-1215 天草市河浦町白木河内175-13
【営】8：30 ～ 17：00 【休】12/30 ～ 1/1
【料】一般200円　高校生150円　小・中学生100円
20名以上の団体は2割引

前景　Front View

グーテンベルク印刷機　Gutenberg Printing Machine

天草本　Amakusa Bon

Amakusa Colegio Museum is located near the place of arrival of Luis de Almeida who propagated Christianity in Amakusa. Colegio is a Catholic seminary established by the Society of Jesus. At Amakusa Colegio, the latest in Western studies was taught. Many books called *Amakusa bon* were the first books printed by the Western printing machine. We can see books such as *Isoho Monogatari* (Aesop's Fables) and *Heike Monogatari* (Tales of the Heike) that were printed by the Gutenberg Printing Machine which is also on display along with a Nanban Folding Screen and an old pipe organ. On the second floor are displays of the Tensho Embassy boys dispatched to Rome as well as a collection of world dolls.

Open: 8:30 ～ 17:00　Closed: 12/30 ～ 1/1
Address: 175-13 Shirakigawachi Kawaura-machi Amakusa-shi Kumamoto-ken 863-1215
Phone: 0969-76-0388

天草ロザリオ館
Amakusa Rosary Museum

71ページも参照

「白秋と共に泊まりし天草の宿はバテレンの宿」の歌碑がある大江は潜伏キリシタンの心静かな里です。小高い丘にそびえる白亜の天主堂は、この地区に脈々と受け継がれた信仰のシンボルです。

そのすぐ下にあるロマネスク調の柔らかな建物が天草ロザリオ館です。天草の「潜伏キリシタン」、「キリスト教解禁後の天草」をテーマにした資料館です。当時の潜伏キリシタンの暮らしや信仰の様子を再現した屋根裏の「隠れ部屋」には、実物大の人形が手を組み、ひざまづきオラショの声が生々しく響き渡っています。

弾圧当時の潜伏キリシタンの信仰対象物マリア観音や葬儀の時に使われた「経消しの壺」など、当時の息遣いまでもが聞こえそうな貴重な信心具が展示されています。

【問】Tel. 0969 － 42 － 5259
〒863-2801 天草市天草町大江 1749
【営】8：30 ～ 17：00 【休】12/30 ～ 1/1
【料】一般 300 円　高校生 200 円　小・中学生 150 円
20 名以上の団体は 2 割引

前景　Front View

隠れ部屋　Hidden Room

経消しの壺　Kyokeshi no Tsubo

Oe is a quiet village where *Kakure Christians* (Hidden Christians) lived. The chalky white Oe Church standing on a hillside is a symbol to the persistent faith of the Hidden Christians. Amakusa Rosary Museum is located at the beginning of the path leading up to the Oe Church. Themes of the museum are Hidden Christians and the period following the Abolishment of Persecution of Christians in 1873. We can see a replica, Hidden Christian praying room. *Maria Kannon* figures (Buddhist Kannon-like Mary figure) and *Kyokeshi no Tsubo* (Jar to extinguish Buddhist prayers) used at funerals, and other Hidden Christian artifacts are also on display.

Open: 8:30 ～ 17:00 Closed: 12／30 ～ 1／1
Address: 1749 Oe Amakusa-machi Amakusa-shi Kumamoto-ken 863-2801
Phone: 0969-42-5259

﨑津資料館みなと屋
Sakitsu Museum Minatoya

　﨑津教会前の旧旅館みなと屋を改築し、展示スペース、休憩スペースを設け、﨑津資料館みなと屋が開館しました。1階には、江戸時代の潜伏キリシタンの指導者「水方」を中心に信仰したメダイや鏡、銭、祈りの言葉であるオラショを展示しています。特に、白蝶貝のメダイはヨーロッパの金属製メダイを模倣して日本人が制作した大変貴重なものです。また、アワビ貝は祈りの時には水を注ぎ、マリアの姿をした紋様を浮かび上がらせて信仰したと言われています。この他、﨑津集落を復元したジオラマでは、昭和中頃の様子を紹介しています。

　2階では﨑津集落と今富集落の土地利用の在り方、交易、景観、人々の暮らしと信仰の様子を展示しています。休憩スペースでは、映像機器により﨑津、今富の四季の様子や自然について放映しています。﨑津の歴史、文化、自然をお楽しみください。

【問】Tel. 0969 - 75 - 9911
　　　〒863-1204 天草市河浦町﨑津463
【営】9：00～17：00 【休】12/30～1/1 【料】無料
【駐車場】　﨑津ガイダンスセンターや﨑津漁協前の駐車場をご利用ください。

前景　Front View

柱の隠しメダイ　Hidden Medal in Pillar

白蝶貝のメダイ
"Medal" of White Lipped Oyster

The old Japanese inn Minatoya in front of the Sakitsu Church was remodeled and opened as the Sakitsu Museum Minatoya. On the first floor are exhibits of Hidden Christian articles relating to the *Mizukata* (Leaders of the Hidden Christians) from the Edo period. These include faith medals, mirrors, coins, and words of prayer. Of paticular interest are medals made from white-lipped pearl oysters shells that were made in imitation of metal European medals. Abalone shells were used in prayer. When water was poured onto the shell the villagers said a Mary-like image would appear in the water. A diorama of the restored Sakitsu village as it was in the mid-Showa era is also on display. On the second floor are exhibits of the villager's faith and lifestyle, scenery, land use, and commerce of Sakitsu and Imatomi. In the break area we can watch a video on the seasonal scenery of Sakitsu and Imatomi. We hope you will enjoy the history, culture, and nature of Sakitsu.

　　　　　Open: 9:00～17:00　Closed: 12/30～1/1
　　　　　Adress: 463 Sakitsu　Kawaura-machi Amakusa-shi Kumamoto-ken 863-1204
　　　　　Admission fee: Free
　　　　　Phone: 0969-75-9911
　　　　　Parking: Sakitsu Village Guidance Center or Fishermen Co-Op

サンタマリア館
Amakusa Chrisaõ Museum

72 ページも参照

雲仙普賢岳を望む四郎ヶ浜ビーチに平成24年8月リニューアルオープンしました。

ここは「タコ街道」の中心地です。ユーモラスな巨大タコのモニュメント「タコ入道」が迎えてくれます。多くのカップルが十字架や巨大タコを背に記念撮影しています。

地元に残る資料を、館主二代にわたって収集した50体のマリア観音、翼を持ったマリア観音、キリシタン手水鉢、多種多様なロザリオなど隠れキリシタンの貴重な遺物300点を展示しています。厳しい禁教時代を信仰のために様々な工夫を凝らして乗り切ってきた隠れキリシタンの熱い思いが伝わってきます。

前景　Front View

翼を持った観音
Kannon With Wing

マリア観音　*Maria-Kannon*

> サンタマリア館は、2017年に閉館しました。現在、主要展示物は天草四郎メモリアルホールに移されています（本書93ページをご参照ください）。

Amakusa Chrisaõ Museum, renovated and reopened in 2012, is located at the Shirogahama Beach with a nice view of Mt. Unzen. A large octopus statue welcomes visitors. The statue symbolizes the "octopus road" for which the area is well known. Many couples take a keepsake photo in front of the statue. This museum displays about 300 valuables, Hidden Christian artifacts. These incude 50 *Maria-Kannon* figures, Christian water bowls, and many kind of rosaries. We can glimpse the lifestyle of the Hidden Christians through these relics.

> The Amakusa Chrisaõ Museum was closed in 2017. Major exhibitions of the Amakusa Chrisaõ Museum were transferred to the Amakusa Shiro Memorial Hall (page 93) and exhibited in the Hall.

苓北町歴史資料館
Reihoku Historical Museum

39ページも参照

富岡半島は雲仙天草国立公園の中にあり、西は天草灘から東シナ海の大海原が拡がり、男性的で雄大な展望が開け、北から東には女性的な袋湾、巴崎、橘湾、さらに対岸に島原半島と雲仙普賢岳を見ることができます。

1637年天草・島原一揆の際、一揆軍に対して徹底抗戦を行った富岡城（復元）が東縁、中央部にあります。

苓北町歴史資料館はこの富岡城二の丸長櫓に平成27年7月にオープンしました。

寺沢氏、山崎氏、戸田氏の三代にわたる築城、修復、破城の歴史や富岡城図、一揆の陣中日記、天草五人衆の志岐系図、志岐城の古陶片など展示。展望テラスから見える巴崎は「小天橋立」と呼ばれ白砂青松の優雅さは旅人の心を慰めてくれます。城内には熊本県富岡ビジターセンターもあります。

【問】Tel. 0969 - 35 - 0712
〒863-2507 天草郡苓北町富岡字本丸2245
【営】9：00～17：00 【休】毎週木曜日（祝・休日の場合はその翌平日）
【料】一般300円　小・中学生100円　20名以上の団体は2割引

全景　Full View

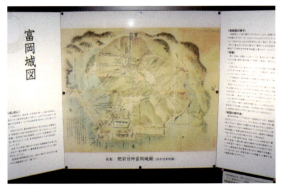

古絵図　Old Picture

薙刀　Old Sword

Tomioka Peninsula located in the Unzen-Amakusa National Park has a view from the Amakusa open sea to the East China Sea in the west, Fukuro Bay, Cape Tomoe, and Tachibana Bay in the north and east. We can see Mt. Unzen over Tachibana Bay. The reconstructed Tomioka Castle is in the center of the Tomioka Peninsula. In 1637, a battle of the Amakusa-Shimabara Rebellion was fought at the former Tomioka Castle. This museum opened in 2015 in a section of the reconstructed Tomioka Castle. The museum displays the history of the castle including old pictures, diaries, ceramics, and other historical items. The Tomioka Visitor Center is located here, too.

Open: 9:00～17:00　Closed: every Thursday
Address: 2245 Honmaru Tomioka Reihoku-machi Amakusa-gun Kumamoto-ken 863-2507
Phone: 0969-35-0712

天草四郎メモリアルホール
Amakusa Shiro Memorial Hall

69ページも参照

天草・島原一揆の折、一揆勢が密議を凝らしたという湯島（談合島）を見渡せる天草四郎公園の一角に聖堂風のメモリアルホールはあります。

天草・島原一揆の一揆勢の総大将として彗星のごとく登場し、若干16歳という短い生涯を終えた謎の美少年「天草四郎時貞」を中心に立体映像、ジオラマ、光、音楽などの手法を使って南蛮文化、キリスト教の伝来、キリスト教徒への弾圧、一揆と殉教の歴史などを分かりやすく伝える体験型の歴史テーマ館です。

ザビエルの等身大の像や実物大の二分の一の南蛮船などがあり、450年前の日本にタイムスリップしたようです。館の上部には幻想的なムードに包まれる瞑想空間もあります。

- 【問】Tel. 0964 - 56 - 5311
  〒869-3603 上天草市大矢野町中977 - 1
- 【営】9：00 ～ 17：00 【休】12/29 ～ 1/1　1月の第2水曜日、6月の第2水曜日
- 【料】一般600円　中学生以下300円（幼児は無料）20名以上の団体は1割引

全景　Full View

天草四郎　Shiro Amakusa

コレジヨの様子　Recreated Scene at Colegio

Amakusa Shiro Memorial Hall, temple-like in appearance, is located at Amakusa Shiro Park which has a view of Yushima island. Yushima island is the place where Shiro Amakusa and his army made battle plans. Yushima island is also called *Dango Jima* which roughly means 'Secret Meeting Island'. Being an extraordinarily charismatic figure, Shiro Amakusa quickly became the leader of the Amakusa-Shimabara Rebellion. He was killed at the young age of 16. This hall displays depictions of Shiro Amakusa, European culture, introduction of Christianity, and the period of persecution of Christianity. The hall shows 3D movies with light rays and music. We can see a statue of St. Francis Xavier and a half-size Western ship. It's like taking a journey 450 years back in time.

Open: 9:00 ～ 17:00 Closed: 12／29 ～ 1/1, second Wednesday of January and June
Address: 977-1 Naka Oyano-machi Kamiamakusa-shi Kumamoto-ken 869-3603
Phone: 0964-56-5311
HP: http://www.kamiamakusa-c.kumamoto-sgn.jp

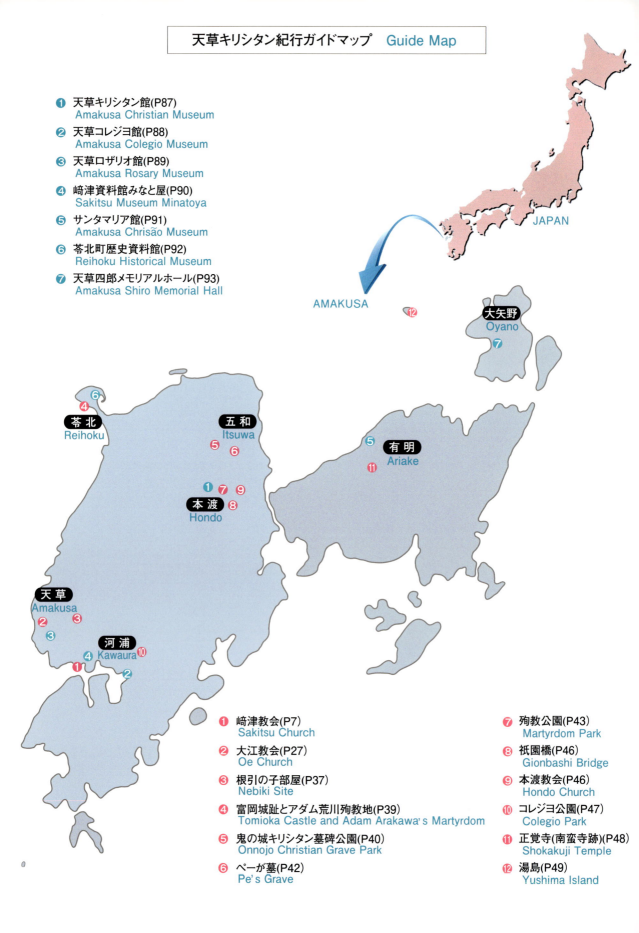

世界遺産「長崎と天草地方の潜伏キリシタン関連遺産」ガイドマップ

　「長崎と天草地方の潜伏キリシタン関連遺産」は、平成30年6月に世界遺産に登録されました。これは、長崎県の長崎市、南島原市、佐世保市、平戸市、五島市、小値賀町、新上五島町そして熊本県天草市の、2県6市2町に点在する12資産で構成されています。「長崎と天草地方の潜伏キリシタン関連遺産」は、キリスト教の禁教期に密かに信仰を継承した『集落』と、これに関連する資産です。これらは、海に面した半島や離島に点在しており、日本においてキリスト教が徹底的に禁じられ、200年以上にわたって宣教師が不在であったにも関わらず、信仰が継承された独特の伝統文化を証明する希有な物証です。

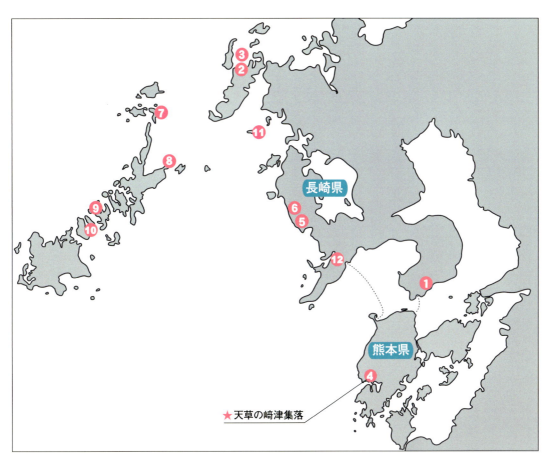

	❶ 原城跡	長崎県南島原市南有馬町
	❷ 平戸の聖地と集落(春日集落と安満岳)	長崎県平戸市春日町
	❸ 平戸の聖地と集落(中江ノ島)	長崎県平戸市下中野町
★	❹ 天草の﨑津集落	熊本県天草市河浦町
	❺ 外海の出津集落	長崎県長崎市下大野町
	❻ 外海の大野集落	長崎県長崎市西出津町
	❼ 野崎島の集落跡	長崎県北松浦郡小値賀町
	❽ 頭ヶ島の集落	長崎県南松浦郡新上五島町
	❾ 奈留島の江上集落	長崎県五島市蕨町
	❿ 久賀島の集落	長崎県五島市奈留町
	⓫ 黒島の集落	長崎県佐世保市黒島町
	⓬ 大浦天主堂	長崎県長崎市南山手町

Guide Map of 「Hidden Christian Sites in the Nagasaki Region」

'Hidden Christian Sites in the Nagasaki Region' has achieved World Heritage Sites in 2018. These Sites are comprised of 12 places in an area that spans from the Goto Islands over to Sasebo, down through Nagasaki City and ending in Amakusa. 'Hidden Christian Sites in the Nagasaki Region' are sites related to the history of Hidden Christian who kept their faith during a long period when Christianity was banned nationwide. These sites are located on islands and peninsulas facing the sea. That the Hidden Christians had kept their faith for over 200 years in the absense of any missionaries is an extraordinary cultural legacy.

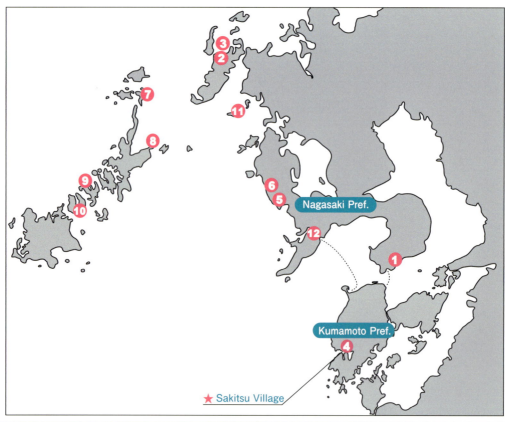

❶	Hara Castle	South Arima, South Shimabara City, Nagasaki Pref.
❷	Kasuga Village and Sacred Places in Hirado (Kasuga Village and Mt.Yasumandake)	Kasuga, Hirado City, Nagasaki Pref.
❸	Kasuga Village and Sacred Places in Hirado (Nakaenoshima Island)	Shimo-Nakano, Hirado City, Nagasaki Pref.
★ ❹	Sakitsu Village in Amakusa	Kawaura, Amakusa City, Kumamoto Pref.
❺	Shitsu Village in Sotome	Shimo-Ono, Nagasaki City, Nagasaki Pref.
❻	Ono Village in Sotome	West Shitsu, Nagasaki City, Nagasaki Pref.
❼	Settlement Sites on Nozaki Island	Ojika, North Matsuura County, Nagasaki Pref.
❽	Settlements in Kashiragashima Island	Shinkamigoto, South Matsuura County, Nagasaki Pref.
❾	Egami Settlement in Naru Island	Warabi, Goto City, Nagasaki Pref.
❿	Settlements in Hisaka Island	Naru, Goto City, Nagasaki Pref.
⓫	Settlements in Kuroshima Island	Kuroshima, Sasebo City, Nagasaki Pref.
⓬	Oura Cathedral	South Yamate, Nagasaki City, Nagasaki Pref.

協力者一覧

本書は下記の方々の格別のご協力により発刊することができました。厚く御礼申し上げます。

敬称略

寄稿	宮原 良治	福岡市在住　カトリック福岡司教区司教 序文「発刊によせて」執筆	
監修	渡辺 隆義	天草市在住　﨑津教会・大江教会・本渡教会主任司祭 監修および「天草の思いを世界に」執筆	
編集	小林 健浩	天草市本渡町本泉７４６－４ 天草フォトクラブ会長　元天草キリシタン館運営委員長	
協力	平田 豊弘	天草市志柿町在住　元天草市世界遺産推進室長　学芸員、天草キリシタン館長 「天草のキリスト教史」、「世界遺産の﨑津集落」、 「天草のキリスト教年表」執筆	
〃	亀子 研二	天草市本渡町在住　元天草キリシタン館長 「資料館の案内」執筆	
〃	永田 隆一	天草市亀場町在住 写真提供および写真レタッチ	
〃	森 祥一	熊本市中央区在住 英訳	
〃	カール ジェンソン Carl Jenson	天草市亀場町在住　アメリカ モンタナ州出身　英会話講師 天草フォトクラブ会員　英訳および写真提供	

また下記の方々にご協力いただきました。厚く御礼申し上げます。

敬称略

山頭 原太郎（やまがしら）	カトリック福岡司教区司祭
川上 栄光（かわうえ）	神言修道会司祭
海付 親治（うみつき）	﨑津教会信徒会元代表
崎本 和人	大江教会信徒会代表
山下 富士夫	﨑津教会信徒会元代表
山下 富浩	河浦町﨑津在住
山下 大惠	天草町大江在住
川嶋 富登喜	河浦町今富在住
川田 富博	河浦町河浦在住
浜崎 献作	天草市有明町在住
川上 謙二	天草市佐伊津町在住　絵画提供
リチャード ブレジナ Dr. Richard Brezina	天草市在住　英訳

そのほか﨑津、大江、本渡の各教会の方々やシスター（方）、および各資料館にご協力いただきました。

Acknowledgements

"Amakusa Christian Sites" has been made possible with support of many people to whom I wish to express my sincere gratitude.

[Contributors]

Ryoji Miyahara	Bishop, Diocese of Fukuoka, wrote "Forward"

[Editorial Supervision]

Takayoshi Watanabe	Parish Priest of Sakitsu, Oe, and Hondo Catholic Churches Editorial Supervisor, wrote "From Amakusa to the World"

[Editing]

Takehiro Kobayashi	President of Amakusa Photo Club, Former Amakusa Christian Museum Operations Chairman, Resides at 746-4 Motoizumi, Hondo, Amakusa City

[Collaborators]

Toyohiro Hirata	Former Director, World Heritage Promotion Section, wrote "Christianity History of Amakusa", "World Heritage of Sakitsu Village" and "Chronology of Christianity in Amakusa"
Kenji Kameko	Wrote "Museum Guide"
Ryuichi Nagata	Provided photographs and photo retouching
Shoichi Mori	Provided preliminary Japanese to English translations
Carl Jenson	English teacher from Montana, USA, member of Amakusa Photo Club, provided photographs and final English translations

I am very grateful to the following people who supported this project.

Gentaro Yamagashira	Priest, Diocese of Fukuoka
Eimitsu Kawaue	Priest, Society of the Divine Word
Chikaharu Umitsuki	Representative of Sakitsu Church parishioners
Kazuto Sakimoto	Representative of Oe Church parishioners
Fujio Yamashita	Advisor
Tomihiro Yamashita	Advisor
Hiroshige Yamashita	Advisor
Futoki Kawashima	Advisor
Tomihiro Kawata	Advisor
Kensaku Hamasaki	Director of Museum, contributed materials
Kenji Kawakami	Contributed pictures
Dr. Richard Brezina	English translations
Others	Many people including Sisters from Sakitsu, Imatomi and Oe

あとがき

　2015年11月23日。鈴木神社（田口孝雄宮司）の例大祭が催行されたが、この日の式典は例年にも増して荘厳で和やかな雰囲気に包まれた。例年の東向寺岡部住職等の高僧に加え、﨑津・大江教会の渡辺神父の穏やかな姿があった。この新たな歴史を飾る天草らしい光景に、大方の参列者は心を打たれ粛々とした気持ちになった。

右から
渡辺神父
円性寺石原住職
田口宮司
信福寺池田住職
東向寺岡部住職

　そこにはまた例年見かける平田室長の姿もあった。そして「写真集をやってもらえませんか」。数年来懇願されていたが、一応普通の仏教徒である私にとって「キリシタン」は、やはり立ち入れない領域であった。

　しかしこの日私の心は決まった。今回は最高のメンバーに恵まれた。渡辺神父の深いご理解による全面的なご協力。今まで禁制だったミサの詳細も撮影が許された。心から感謝致します。平田室長は当初から天草における世界遺産の推進役で、学芸員の専門的知識に加え﨑津・大江に熟知されている。今なお世界遺産登録を目指しての奮闘が続いている。亀子氏は長年天草キリシタン館長を務め、天草のキリシタン事情について精通しておられる。カール・ジェンソン氏は我が写真の友であり、英語の師でもある。今回目を見張るドローン撮影と英訳で活躍いただいた。また永田氏には写真のレタッチを何度もしていただいた。そして旧友で秀才の森祥一氏にも英訳で助太刀いただいた。

　この本の発刊が決まってから﨑津や大江には30回以上撮影や取材で出かけた。その都度信者さんの温かくて純粋な気持ちに触れることができた。強い信仰が日ごろの暮らしの中に息づいていることも実感できた。そしていつも清々しい気持ちになり、恩返しは良い本に仕上げることと自分に誓いながら帰途についていた。天草の誇る﨑津教会や大江教会の美しい佇まいの裏には過去の不幸な歴史や信者の方々の深い信仰が隠されていることをぜひ実感していただきたいと願います。

　今回の本は多くの人の力を結集して出来上がった。また本書に登場いただいた方々など大勢の関係者の方にもご協力いただいた。特に弦書房の小野社長には快く出版を引き受けていただいた。心から感謝申し上げます。

　この半年の間に、世界遺産の申請の延期という不運と熊本地震という強烈な天災に見舞われた。早い時期の世界遺産への登録と熊本の力強い復興を願って本書を捧げます。　　2016年6月　小林　健浩

〔補記〕「天草の﨑津集落」は、「長崎と天草地方の潜伏キリシタン関連遺産」の構成資産の一つとして、2018年6月世界文化遺産に登録されました。

Epilogue

November 23rd, 2015 was a fine day at the Autumn Festival of the Suzuki Shrine. Chief priest Takao Taguchi conducted the festival in a magnificent and friendly atmosphere. Even though it was a Shinto ceremony, Mr. Okabe the chief priest of the Tokoji Temple and Father Watanabe of Sakitsu and Oe Churches were in attendance. Those attending the festival were moved to see this new chapter in Amakusa history. Mr. Hirata was there as usual. He approached me with the suggestion that I publish a photo collection of Christianity in Amakusa. Since I myself am not a Christian but an ordinary Buddhist, I was apprehensive. But talking with many great people there inspired me and I made up my mind that I would move forward in my endeavor to create this book. I am most grateful to Father Watanabe for his generosity and understanding, allowing me to take pictures at Mass which is usually prohibited. Mr. Hirata has expert knowledge as a curator and is familiar with the Sakitsu and Oe area. He works diligently to realize the dream of getting the Sakitsu Church registered as a World Heritage Site. Mr. Kameko worked for many years as director of the Amakusa Christian Museum and has profound knowledge of Christianity in Amakusa. Carl Jenson is my photography friend and English teacher. He has provided amazing aerial drone photos and English translations. Mr. Nagata has supported me with color adjustments. Mr. Mori, my high school friend has provided preliminary English translations.

Since that day when I decided I would put forth this book I have been to the Oe and Sakitsu Churches over 30 times taking pictures and covering events. Every time I met with Christians I was touched by their warmth and genuineness. I have gained a true sense of the strong faith they hold as they go about their daily lives. On my way home I always felt reenergized and promised myself I would repay them with my best work. I hope the reader will realize not only the majestic beauty of Amakusa's pride-the Oe and Sakitsu Churches, but also the sad history beneath, through which Amakusa Christians were forced to hide their faith.

This book has been made possible by the efforts and contributions of many people. I especially would like to thank President Ono of Genshobo, with whom it was a pleasure to work. During the past half year, the Sakitsu Church's registration for World Heritage Site has been postponed, and we experienced a major disaster in the Great Kumamoto Earthquake. I put forth this book in the dual hopes that the Sakitsu Church will soon become a World Heritage Site and that Kumamoto will make a solid recovery.

June 2016   Takehiro Kobayashi

Supplement: The Sakitsu Village in Amakusa was registered as one component of Hidden Christian Sites in the Nagasaki Region in June 2018.

〈編者略歴〉
小林健浩（こばやし・たけひろ）
昭和18年（1943）8月天草市浄南町生まれ
本渡北小学校、本渡中学校卒業
昭和37年（1962）天草高校卒業
昭和39年（1964）久留米工業短期大学電気工学科卒業
同年早川電機工業株式会社（現シャープ株式会社）入社
平成6年（1994）帰郷し写真活動開始
著書　『天草潮風紀行』『天草写真風土記』『天草一〇〇景』（以上、弦書房）
（現住所）
〒863‐0004
熊本県天草市本渡町本泉746‐4
（所属）
天草フォトクラブ会長
熊日フォト・サークル運営委員
天草文化協会会員

天草キリシタン紀行
崎津・大江・キリシタンゆかりの地

2016年10月30日第1刷発行
2018年8月20日第3刷発行

　　監　修　　崎津・大江・本渡教会主任司祭　渡辺隆義
　　編　者　　小林健浩
　　発行者　　小野静男
　　発行所　　弦書房
　　　　　　〒810‐0041　福岡市中央区大名2-2-43ELK大名ビル301
　　　　　　TEL 092-726-9885　FAX 092-726-9886
　　　　　　E-mail:books@genshobo.com
　　　　　　http://genshobo.com/

　　印　刷　アロー印刷株式会社
　　製　本　篠原製本株式会社

ⓒ 2016
無断転載を禁じます
落丁・乱丁本はお取替えいたします
ISBN978-4-86329-142-3　C0026

◆弦書房の本◆　　　　　　　　　　　　　　　＊表示価格は税別

かくれキリシタンの起源
信仰と信者の実相

中園成生　現在も継承される信仰の全容を明らかにし、なぜ長年の「かくれキリシタン」論争に終止符を打つ。従来のイメージをくつがえし、四〇〇年間変わらず継承された信仰の実像に迫る。〈A5判・504頁〉4000円

●FUKUOKA Uブックレット❾
かくれキリシタンとは何か
オラショを巡る旅

中園成生　四〇〇年間変わらなかった信仰──現在も続くかくれキリシタン信仰の歴史とその真の姿に迫るフィールドワーク。かくれキリシタン信者は、それまで伝えてきたキリシタン信仰の形を、忠実に継承することしかできなかった【2刷】〈A5判・64頁〉680円

【評伝】天草五十人衆

天草学研究会【編】〈島〉であり〈天領〉であった天草は、独特の歴史を刻み、多くの異能の人々を生み出した。天草四郎から吉本隆明まで、天草スピリッツを体現した50人の足跡から、この島がもつ歴史の多面性に迫る。【3刷】〈A5判・320頁〉2400円

熊本の近代化遺産 [上][下]

熊本産業遺産研究会・熊本まちなみトラスト編　明治日本の産業革命遺産（世界遺産推薦）の構成資産のうち「三角港」「万田坑」の二つの遺産を含む一四〇の近代化遺産群を上下巻で紹介。カラー写真と詳細な解説付。〈A5判・176頁〉各1900円

ここすぎて 水の径

石牟礼道子　著者が66歳（一九九三年）から74歳（二〇〇一年）の円熟期に書かれた長期連載エッセイをまとめた一冊。後に『苦海浄土』『天湖』『アニマの鳥』など数々の名作を生んだ著者の思想と行動の源流へと誘う珠玉のエッセイ47篇。〈四六判・320頁〉2400円

もうひとつのこの世
石牟礼道子の宇宙

渡辺京二　〈石牟礼文学〉の特異な独創性が渡辺京二によって発見されて半世紀。互いに触発される日々の中から生まれた〈石牟礼道子論〉を集成。石牟礼文学の豊かさとときわだつ特異性を著者独自の視点から明快に解きあかす。〈四六判・232頁〉2200円